How Glooskap Found Summer

and Other Curious Tales

Retold by Lynne Benton
Illustrated by Kristen Guerin

A Harcourt Achieve Imprint

www.Rigby.com
1-800-531-5015

Literacy by Design Leveled Readers: *How Glooskap Found Summer and Other Curious Tales*

ISBN-13: 978-1-4189-3911-3
ISBN-10: 1-4189-3911-0

© 2008 Harcourt Achieve Inc.

All rights reserved. No part of the material protected by this copyright may be reproduced or utilized in any form or by any means, in whole or in part, without permission in writing from the copyright owner. Requests for permission should be mailed to: Paralegal Department, 6277 Sea Harbor Drive, Orlando, FL 32887.

Rigby is a trademark of Harcourt Achieve Inc.

Printed in China
4 5 6 7 8 0940 14 13 12 11 10 09

Contents

Why Mosquitoes Buzz
in One's Ears
A Tale from Africa

Long ago, Mosquito didn't buzz–he
talked. He liked the sound of his own
voice so much that he talked on and
on, until the other animals grew tired of
listening and did their best to avoid him.

But one day Mosquito flew up to
Lizard before he could escape and said,
"Oh, I'm glad I caught you, Lizard,
because I wanted to tell you all about my
vacation."

"You've told me," sighed Lizard,
"several times."

Mosquito took no notice and continued,
"Well, there I was, lying on the beach,
and . . . "

He went on, and on, and on.

After an hour, Lizard yawned and said, "Mosquito, I'm sorry, but I must go."

"Wait," said Mosquito, "I'm just coming to the best part!"

Lizard had heard the best part several times and decided he couldn't bear to hear it again. Clapping his feet to his ears, he ran off into the jungle, screaming.

Snake, who lay asleep in the weeds, heard Lizard's scream and woke up in a fright.

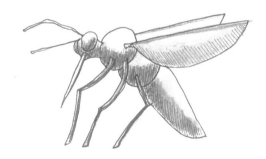

"Something dreadful must have happened! I'd better hide!" he thought and slid quickly down the nearest hole.

The nearest hole, however, belonged to Rabbit, and when Rabbit saw Snake crawling down into his burrow, he was so terrified that he shot out of the other entrance and raced off through the trees.

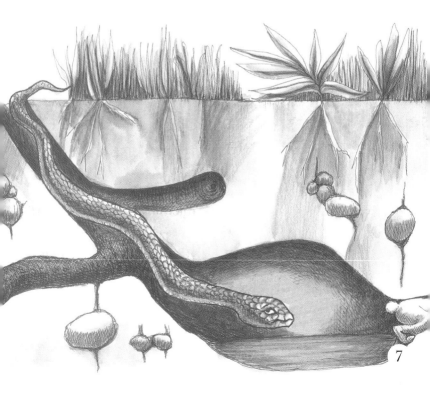

Crow, gliding overhead, spotted Rabbit running and thought to himself, "There must be danger, so I should warn the others." Crow flew over the jungle, calling at the top of his voice, "Danger, danger, run for your lives!"

Monkey heard Crow above him. He jumped up in alarm and swung through the branches, searching for a safe place where danger couldn't reach him.

It was just bad luck that Monkey landed on a branch where Owl was sitting on her nest, guarding her eggs. Poor Owl, shocked out of a comfortable sleep, jumped in fright, and her nest fell from the branch.

Both Owl and Monkey watched in horror as Owl's eggs fell toward the ground.

"My chicks!" screeched Owl, and she frantically flapped her wings.

Monkey was very upset and quickly apologized. "Oh, Owl! Your eggs! Please, please let me help you! Here—I'll pick them up!"

Owl continued to flap her wings. Monkey felt more distressed than ever and tried to explain that he was only trying to escape from danger.

As the two of them carefully checked the eggs for cracks, Owl asked, "Danger? What danger?"

"I'm not sure," said Monkey, "but it was Crow who called out a warning, so I'll ask him."

Monkey swung back up into the trees until he saw Crow and asked, "Crow, what is the danger?"

"I don't know," replied Crow, shaking his head. "I saw Rabbit running away from something, so I thought there *must* be danger. We'd better ask him."

They both hurried on until they saw Rabbit hiding under a bush.

"What were you running from?" asked Monkey and Crow.

"I was escaping from Snake," Rabbit said, "because he came sliding into my burrow!"

"Then perhaps we'd better ask him," said Monkey.

So Monkey went to the other entrance to Rabbit's burrow, where he found Snake, who was trying to back out of the hole.

"Why did you go into Rabbit's burrow, Snake?" asked Monkey.

"It'sss not my fault," hissed Snake. "I heard Lizard scream, so I slid down the nearest hole. I didn't know it was Rabbit's."

"Well, we'd better find Lizard and see what all this business is about," Monkey insisted.

Spotting Lizard under a nearby tree, Monkey went up to him and demanded, "Can you please tell me, Lizard, what happened that caused you to upset the whole jungle?"

"What do you mean?" asked Lizard. He looked puzzled.

So Monkey explained that Lizard's scream had frightened Snake, who had terrified Rabbit, who had worried Crow, who had startled him, so that he'd landed on Owl's branch and knocked all her eggs to the ground. Then he said, "So, Lizard, what we want to know is, what exactly *is* the danger?"

Lizard stared at Monkey bewildered, then he smiled knowingly and answered, "Oh, there was never any danger. Mosquito just wouldn't stop talking, so I screamed, that's all."

"That's *all*?" shouted the animals, and they turned on Mosquito. "So it's all *your* fault!" they accused.

Mosquito was so shocked that for once he found that he couldn't speak. The animals left him and went back to try to help Owl repair her nest.

Owl usually took days and days to build a nest. But she and Monkey and Crow and Lizard and Rabbit worked as quickly as they could to put the damaged nest back together. Even Snake helped by carefully wrapping himself around Owl's eggs to keep them warm. After many hours, the animals managed to rebuild a nest for Owl's eggs that was as good as new.

But the animals had to take their time. They had to work all through the night. They couldn't have just slapped together any old nest. It was important that it be

sturdy and snug, so the eggs could again be kept safe and warm. Snake was doing a fine job for the moment, but he couldn't be expected to lie still forever, making sure that the eggs were nice and cozy.

The animals finished the new nest in the early hours of the morning, and all of them were very tired. Their heads nodded, their eyelids drooped, and Monkey and Lizard even began to snore a little.

Snake, however, began to shiver. He had no fur like Monkey or Rabbit with which to keep himself warm. And having to lie so still while wrapped around the delicate eggs meant that he couldn't warm himself by moving around all night like Owl and Crow and Lizard. The hour was getting late, and this was the jungle, after all. Snake had grown used to the sun coming up and keeping things nice and toasty.

He called out, "Owl, exsssscussse me. I know you're very tired, but I'm shhhivering! Would you please hoot for the sun? It's getting late, and I'm growing colder by the second. If I freeze, how can I possibly keep your eggs warm?"

"Yes, Owl," the others agreed. "Please hoot for the sun."

Owl hooted three times, and the sky began to brighten.

The sun began to rise, and golden light filtered through the leaves. The animals thought the jungle had never

looked so beautiful.

"Thank you, Owl," the animals said. Monkey carefully placed Owl's eggs in the nest, and Owl settled gently down upon them. "Thank you for calling the sun."

But when Mosquito tried to say "thank you" too, the words wouldn't come out; the only sound he could make was a tiny buzz.

And to this day, mosquitoes have not been able to speak a single word. They can only buzz in one's ears, as if to say, "I'm so sorry!"

How Glooskap Found Summer
A Native American Legend

Once, long ago, the land of the Wawaniki people was always warm, crops grew well in the fertile soil, and food was plentiful. The people were happy.

But then something changed. It turned bitterly cold, and food became scarce as snow covered the rock-hard ground. Ice formed on the lakes and rivers, and the people huddled around their fires shivering and wondering what they had done wrong.

Their leader, a wise man called Glooskap, was desperate to help his people before they suffered any more from cold and hunger, but he had no idea how to do it.

Then one morning Glooskap saw a huge bird with a golden crest and silver-tipped wings circling overhead. Glooskap had never seen anything like it before, but several men were already raising their bows and arrows.

Glooskap cried, "Stop! Don't hurt it! This is no normal bird."

"But our families are starving," protested the men.

"One bird will not feed you all, even a bird as big as that," he said frowning. "Perhaps if we were to spare its life, our fortunes would change."

The men grumbled, but they admired Glooskap, so they lowered their bows as the bird landed in front of them.

Suddenly, to everyone's astonishment, the bird spoke up. "Thank you for not causing me harm, because I have come to help you."

"If you can tell us how to free our land from this terrible cold, you will indeed be a great help to us," said Glooskap.

"You must travel north," said the bird, "to find the great giant, Winter, who has frozen your land with his icy breath. He wishes to claim your land, but if you were to persuade him to leave you alone, he might agree."

Glooskap thanked the bird, saying, "I will leave immediately!"

"And I will take you there," said the bird. Glooskap said farewell to his people and climbed onto the bird's back.

For a day and a night they flew north, until they reached a land covered with thick ice and deep, deep snow. Here the bird stopped and said, "I cannot fly any farther, but do you see that great wigwam on the horizon? That is where the giant Winter lives. You must demand that he leave your land, so that your crops will grow again and your people can eat."

"I will do my best," said Glooskap, shivering, "and thank you for bringing me here. If I succeed, the Wawaniki people will always be grateful to you."

As the bird bowed its gold-crested head, lifted its silver-tipped wings, and flew away, Glooskap squared his shoulders and marched on toward the great wigwam on the horizon.

When he reached it, Glooskap called out, "Giant Winter, it is I, Glooskap, of the Wawaniki people. May I come in and speak with you?"

A deep voice replied, "Come in, Glooskap of the Wawaniki, and welcome."

So Glooskap took a deep breath and went in.

In front of Glooskap, on a huge icy throne, sat Winter. He was so enormous that Glooskap reached only as high as his knee, but he could see the giant's face, pale as milk, the icicles glittering in his silver-white beard, and his deep, dark eyes that seemed to pierce right through Glooskap.

Glooskap felt very small, and quite terrified, yet the knowledge that his people relied upon him gave him strength. Bowing his head, he said, "Winter, I am honored to meet you."

The giant laughed a great, booming laugh that filled the air, and said, "Don't be afraid, little man, but come, sit here by me."

So Glooskap did as he was told–but before he could make his request, Winter said, "Let me tell you about my country." And in a surprisingly gentle voice, the giant began to talk about his beautiful, silent land where ice and snow lay on the ground all year round. Glooskap felt himself getting warmer and more relaxed, finally falling into a deep, magical sleep.

When Glooskap woke, he wondered for a moment where he was. He looked around and saw that the huge throne of ice was now empty. His heart sank, for he realized that Winter had gotten the better of him. He had no idea how long he had been asleep, but he was afraid it had been a long, long time. "My people must think I have deserted them," he thought, and he hoped they hadn't suffered terribly from the cold.

Leaping to his feet, Glooskap hurried
outside and looked around for the giant.
There was no sign of him, but when
Glooskap looked up, he saw the golden-
crested bird with silver-tipped wings
circling above his head.

"Oh, I am so glad to see you, bird," he
cried, nearly weeping with joy.
"How long have I been under the
giant's spell?"

The bird landed gracefully in front
of him and said, "You must be very
strong because you have slept for only six
months, whereas most of Winter's victims
sleep for a year or more."

"But do you have news of my people?"
cried Glooskap worriedly.

"They miss you," the bird said gravely, "because it is desperately cold and many are very hungry, but they still trust that you will help them."

Glooskap shook his head sadly and said, "I have achieved nothing, so maybe I should go back and let my people choose a new leader."

"Nonsense!" said the bird. "I have another suggestion."

Glooskap looked up. "You mean all is not yet lost?" he asked.

"No," said the bird, "there is another one, luckily, who is even greater than the giant Winter. Her name is Summer, and if you ask her, she may help you defeat Winter."

"Where can I find her?" asked Glooskap eagerly.

"She lives a long way to the south," said the bird, "in a land where the sun always shines, and fruits and flowers grow in great numbers."

"It sounds wonderful," said Glooskap. "Can you take me there?"

"Certainly," said the bird, and once again Glooskap climbed onto the bird's back. They flew away from the cold north toward warmth and sunshine.

After two days and nights, Glooskap and the bird reached the blue southern ocean where the weather was warm and the air rich with the scents of spices and fragrant flowers. At last the bird came to rest on a sandy beach dotted with palm trees, and Glooskap thought it was the most beautiful place he had ever seen.

As Glooskap climbed off the bird's back, he saw a beautiful, glowing woman dancing on the sand, her long brown hair crowned with bright flowers.

Glooskap hurried toward her and said, "I am Glooskap, leader of the Wawaniki, and I have come a long way to find Summer."

"Then you have found her," the woman said, laughing, "for I am Summer. What can I do for you?"

Glooskap explained that Winter had taken over his land, so that no crops would grow and people were suffering from the bitter cold.

Summer listened, and then she said, "Winter can be cruel, but you must stand up to him."

"I tried," said Glooskap, "but he put a spell on me, and I slept for six months."

"Only six months!" Summer marveled, adding, "Then you must be very strong! Well, I'll tell you what I will do. I will come back with you to Winter's homeland, but you must face him alone, because your people will respect you more if you defeat him yourself."

"But how can I stop him from making me fall asleep again?" asked Glooskap doubtfully.

"*You* must do all the talking," Summer said, "and if he should try to interrupt, don't let him."

So the bird flew Glooskap and Summer back to Winter's wigwam in the frozen north.

When the trio arrived, Summer waited outside while Glooskap once again cried out, "Giant Winter, it is I, Glooskap of the Wawaniki people, and I wish to speak with you."

Once again Winter replied, "Come in, Glooskap of the Wawaniki, and welcome."

But this time, as soon as Glooskap entered, he began to tell Winter all about his own country, and each time Winter tried to interrupt, Glooskap talked more loudly and added more and more details to his story.

Soon Winter's snow-white face became rosy red. Sweat began to pour off it, and the icicles in his beard began to melt. Then Winter realized that his spell wasn't working.

As Winter's wigwam began to melt away as well, Glooskap saw that Summer was using her powers on Winter's kingdom, because patches of green grass showed through the snow, and as the ice melted, the rivers began to run freely again.

Winter wept to see his power leaving him.

Then Summer said, "Now, Winter, you
have seen that my power is greater than
yours, but we might strike a bargain.
If I should promise never to disturb
your own land here, you must agree to
rule over Glooskap's country for only six
months of the year and to be less severe.
Then, for the next six months, I will rule,
so that the people may enjoy the sunshine
and grow their food. During my reign,
they will learn to store food so they may
eat during your reign, and they will

know that I will always return. Do we have a bargain?"

Winter was forced to agree. Glooskap also agreed, glad to know that Winter would not rule his land forever. He understood that it would be wise for his people to save food in times of plenty to provide for times when food was scarce.

"Thank you, Summer," Glooskap said, "for now I can return to my people and prepare them for what will be."

So the huge bird flew Glooskap back to his people, who rejoiced at his return. And ever since, Winter has ruled over Glooskap's country for six months of every year and is always followed by six months of glorious Summer.

Why Kangaroos Have Pouches
A Story from Australia

Long ago kangaroos had no way to keep track of their babies, so they were always losing them because their babies are very small.

One day Kangaroo was searching for her son Joey. Seeing a movement in the gum tree, she bounded toward it, but it was only the wind shaking the leaves.

"Why don't you look where you're going?" shouted an angry voice at Kangaroo's feet.

Kangaroo looked down to see a fat, old, angry wombat. "You nearly knocked me over!" Wombat grumbled.

"I'm sorry," said Kangaroo, "but I didn't see you. I've lost my baby, Joey, and I must find him."

"Hmmph," muttered Wombat. "Kids today! No consideration! That's right, go off and leave me," Wombat continued to grumble. "How I'm going to find good grass to eat, I don't know. Nearly blind, I am, but what concern is that of yours?"

Kangaroo paused, for although she was anxious to find Joey, she felt sorry for poor Wombat. "If you climb on to my tail," she said, "I'll take you to some good grass."

Immediately Wombat held on to Kangaroo's strong tail, and she hopped away to a big meadow full of lush green grass.

When they arrived, Wombat wasn't even a little bit grateful. He complained, "You went too fast, and now I'm out of breath!"

"I'm sorry," said Kangaroo, as Wombat grumbled and waddled off to eat the good green grass.

Kangaroo looked around the meadow, but sadly, she couldn't see Joey there either. She was beginning to worry. If little Joey climbed a tree, he might not be able to get down. Or if he fell in the river, he might drown. What if hunters were to find him?

Then Wombat said, "Now I need some water."

Kangaroo sighed. Wombat was a very demanding animal, yet Kangaroo didn't want to leave him on his own, knowing he couldn't see very well.

"Climb onto my tail again, then," Kangaroo said, "and I'll take you to the water hole."

"Mind that you don't go too fast this time," said Wombat. "My old bones don't like being shaken around!"

"I won't," said Kangaroo, and she hopped slowly and carefully all the way to the water hole.

Wombat climbed off Kangaroo's tail and went to take a cool drink. Kangaroo, to her joy, suddenly spotted Joey standing on the edge of the pool, looking down into the water.

"Joey," she cried, "there you are!"

Joey turned, and when he saw his mother, he squealed, "Mom!" and leaped happily toward her.

Then Kangaroo noticed some men in the distance. They were heading toward the water hole, too, carrying long spears.

With alarm, she thought, "Hunters—and they're coming this way!"

Joey jumped into Kangaroo's arms, squeaking, "I'm frightened!" and Kangaroo held him close.

"Quickly, we must hide!" she said, backing into the gum trees.

Then Kangaroo realized that Wombat was still drinking from the water hole, unaware of the approaching hunters. She called, "Come with us, Wombat. The hunters are coming and we must hide!"

Wombat grumbled, but he left the water hole and joined Kangaroo and Joey in the bushes, where they hid and remained very quiet until the hunters had drunk their fill of water and gone on their way.

Then Kangaroo dared to breathe again. "Are you all right, Joey?" she asked, and Joey nodded happily. But when she looked around for Wombat, to her surprise, he had vanished.

"Where did he go?" she asked, but Joey didn't know.

And then, quite suddenly, a tall figure appeared. He wore a splendid brown cloak, and he had a kind and gentle face. He held nothing in his hand.

Kangaroo stared at him in amazement and then she asked, "Who are you?"

"I," said the man, "am the protector of all creatures, and I disguised myself as a wombat and came to find the kindest animal in the land."

Astonished, Kangaroo tried to think who was the kindest animal she knew. "Have you found the kindest animal?" she asked at last.

The protector of all creatures smiled and said, "I certainly have. You, Kangaroo, were worried about young Joey here, but still you bothered with a grumpy old Wombat. He was cross and ungrateful, but you took care of him and you didn't once complain, so I think you are the kindest animal in the land."

Kangaroo was so surprised at this unexpected praise that she didn't know what to say.

Then the protector of all creatures said, "So I am going to give you a special gift." He took some bark off a tree and said, "Tie this around your waist."

Kangaroo did as he asked, and to her amazement, the bark turned into a furry pouch that became part of her body.

"Now you have a way to keep your son safe," said the protecor of all creatures.

Joey was so delighted that he hopped right into the pouch and exclaimed, "Now I won't get lost anymore!"

"Thank you," said Kangaroo softly. "It's just what I need." Then she added, "If only all my friends could have pouches, too!"

The protector of all creatures smiled again and said, "Kangaroo, you are definitely the kindest of all animals, and you shall have your wish."

And today that is why kangaroos and many other animals have pouches in which to carry their babies.